SERIES

A NavPress Bible study on the book of

2 TIMOTHY

D1298694

NAVPRESS

A MINISTRY OF THE NAVIGATORS
P.O. Box 6000, Colorado Springs, CO 80934

OUR GUARANTEE TO YOU

The Navigators is an international Christian organization. Our mission is to reach, disciple, and equip people to know Christ and to make Him known through successive generations. We envision multitudes of diverse people in the United States and every other nation who have a passionate love for Christ, live a lifestyle of sharing Christ's love, and multiply spiritual laborers among those without Christ.

NavPress is the publishing ministry of The Navigators. NavPress publications help believers learn biblical truth and apply what they learn to their lives and ministries. Our mission is to stimulate spiritual formation among our readers.

Printed in the United States of America

2 3 4 5 6 7 8 9 10 11 12 13 / 05 04 03 02 01 00 99

CONTENTS

ACKNOWLEDGMENTS

This LifeChange study has been produced through the coordinated efforts of a team of Navigator Bible study developers and NavPress editorial staff, along with a nationwide network of field-testers.

SERIES EDITOR: KAREN LEE-THORP

HOW TO USE THIS STUDY

Objectives

Each guide in the LIFECHANGE series of Bible studies covers one book of the
Bible. Although the LIFECHANGE guides vary with the individual books they
explore, they share some common goals:
1. To provide you with a firm foundation of understanding and a thirst to
return to the book;
2. To teach you by example how to study a book of the Bible without structured guides;
3. To give you all the historical background, word definitions, and explana-
tory notes you need, so that your only other reference is the Bible;
4. To help you grasp the message of the book as a whole;
5. To teach you how to let God's Word transform you into Christ's image.
Each lesson in this study is designed to take 60 to 90 minutes to complete
on your own. The guide is based on the assumption that you are completing one
lesson per week, but if time is limited you can do half a lesson per week or whatever amount allows you to be thorough.

Flexibility

LIFECHANGE guides are flexible, allowing you to adjust the quantity and depth of
your study to meet your individual needs. The guide offers many optional questions in addition to the regular numbered questions. The optional questions,
which appear in the margins of the study pages, include the following:
Optional Application. Nearly all application questions are optional; we hope
you will do as many as you can without overcommitting yourself.
For Thought and Discussion. Beginning Bible students should be able to
handle these, but even advanced students need to think about them. These
questions frequently deal with ethical issues and other biblical principles. They
often offer cross-references to spark thought, but the references do not give

5

obvious answers. They are good for group discussions.

For Further Study. These include: a) cross-references that shed light on a topic the book discusses, and b) questions that delve deeper into the passage. You can omit them to shorten a lesson without missing a major point of the passage.

(Note: At the end of lessons two through eight you are given the option of outlining the passage just studied. Although the outline is optional, you will probably find it worthwhile.)

If you are meeting in a group, decide together which optional questions to prepare for each lesson, and how much of the lesson you will cover at the next meeting. Normally, the group leader should make this decision, but you might let each member choose his or her own application questions.

As you grow in your walk with God, you will find the LIFECHANGE guide growing with you—a helpful reference on a topic, a continuing challenge for application, a source of questions for many levels of growth.

Overview and Details

The guide begins with an overview of the book. The key to interpretation is context—what is the whole passage or book *about*?—and the key to context is purpose—what is the author's *aim* for the whole work? In lesson one you will lay the foundation for your study by asking yourself, Why did the author (and God) write the book? What did they want to accomplish? What is the book about?

Then, in lesson two, you will begin analyzing successive passages in detail. Thinking about how a paragraph fits into the overall goal of the book will help you to see its purpose. Its purpose will help you see its meaning. Frequently reviewing a chart or outline of the book will enable you to make these connections.

Finally, in the last lesson, you will review the whole book, returning to the big picture to see whether your view of it has changed after closer study. Review will also strengthen your grasp of major issues and give you an idea of how you have grown from your study.

Kinds of Questions

Bible study on your own—without a structured guide—follows a progression. First you observe: What does the passage *say*? Then you interpret: What does the passage *mean*? Lastly you apply: How does this truth affect my life?

Some of the "how" and "why" questions will take some creative thinking, even prayer, to answer. Some are opinion questions without clearcut right answers; these will lend themselves to discussions and side studies.

Don't let your study become an exercise of knowledge alone. Treat the passage as God's Word, and stay in dialogue with Him as you study. Pray, "Lord, what do you want me to see here?" "Father, why is this true?" "Lord, how does this apply to my life?"

It is important that you write down your answers. The act of writing clarifies your thinking and helps you to remember.

Meditating on verses is an option in several lessons. Its purpose is to let biblical truth sink into your inner convictions so that you will increasingly be able to act on this truth as a natural way of life. You may want to find a quiet place to spend five minutes each day repeating the verse(s) to yourself. Think about what each word, phrase, and sentence means to you. At intervals throughout the rest of the day, remind yourself of the verse(s).

Study Aids

A list of reference materials, including a few notes of explanation to help you make good use of them, begins on page 81. This guide is designed to include enough background to let you interpret with just your Bible and the guide. Still, if you want more information on a subject or want to study a book on your own, try the references listed.

Scripture Versions

Unless otherwise indicated, the Bible quotations in this guide are from the New International Version of the Bible. Other versions cited are the Revised Standard Version (RSV), the New American Standard Bible (NASB), and the King James Version (KJV).

Use any translation you like for study, preferably more than one. A paraphrase such as The Living Bible is not accurate enough for study, but it can be helpful for comparison or devotional reading.

Memorizing and Meditating

A Psalmist wrote, "I have hidden your word in my heart that I might not sin against you" (Psalm 119:11). If you write down a verse or passage that challenges or encourages you, and reflect on it often for a week or more, you will find it beginning to affect your motives and actions. We forget quickly what we read once; we remember what we ponder.

When you find a significant verse or passage, you might copy it onto a card to keep with you. Set aside five minutes during each day just to think about what the passage might mean in your life. Recite it over to yourself, exploring its meaning. Then, return to your passage as often as you can during your day, for a brief review. You will soon find it coming to mind spontaneously.

For Group Study

A group of four to ten people allows the richest discussions, but you can adapt this guide for other sized groups. It will suit a wide range of group types, such as home Bible studies, growth groups, youth groups, and businessmen's studies.

Both new and experienced Bible students, and new and mature Christians, will benefit from the guide. You can omit or leave for later years any questions you find too easy or too hard.

The guide is intended to lead a group through one lesson per week. However, feel free to split lessons if you want to discuss them more thoroughly. Or, omit some questions in a lesson if preparation or discussion time is limited. You can always return to this guide for personal study later. You will be able to discuss only a few questions at length, so choose some for discussion and others for background. Make time at each discussion for members to ask about anything they didn't understand.

Each lesson in the guide ends with a section called "For the group." These sections give advice on how to focus a discussion, how you might apply the lesson in your group, how you might shorten a lesson, and so on. The group leader should read each "For the group" at least a week ahead so that he or she can tell the group how to prepare for the next lesson.

Each member should prepare for a meeting by writing answers for all the background and discussion questions to be covered. If the group decides not to take an hour per week for private preparation, then expect to take at least two meetings per lesson to work through the questions. Application will be very difficult, however, without private thought and prayer.

Two reasons for studying in a group are accountability and support. When each member commits in front of the rest to seek growth in an area of life, you can pray with one another, listen jointly for God's guidance, help one another to resist temptation, assure each other that the other's growth matters to you, use the group to practice spiritual principles, and so on. Pray about one another's commitments and needs at most meetings. Spend the first few minutes of each meeting sharing any results from applications prompted by previous lessons. Then discuss new applications toward the end of the meeting. Follow such sharing with prayer for these and other needs.

If you write down each other's applications and prayer requests, you are more likely to remember to pray for them during the week, ask about them at the next meeting, and notice answered prayers. You might want to get a notebook for prayer requests and discussion notes.

Notes taken during discussion will help you to remember, follow up on ideas, stay on the subject, and clarify a total view of an issue. But don't let note-taking keep you from participating. Some groups choose one member at each meeting to take notes. Then someone copies the notes and distributes them at the next meeting. Rotating these tasks can help include people. Some groups have someone take notes on a large pad of paper or erasable marker board (preformed shower wallboard works well), so that everyone can see what has been recorded.

Page 83 lists some good sources of counsel for leading group studies. The *Small Group Letter,* published by NavPress, is unique, offering insights from experienced leaders each month.

BACKGROUND

Paul and Timothy

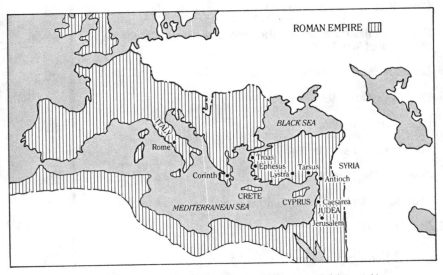

When Paul wrote the letter we call 2 Timothy, he was an old man in a Roman prison. This man who had been Christ's greatest missionary for thirty years was now chained to a Roman guard at all times and awaited a death sentence from the emperor.

Timothy may have been in Ephesus, but in whatever city, he was carrying on the ministry Paul had begun but could not continue. Timothy had been working with Paul for over fifteen years, but now the apostle was departing for good. This charge Timothy received is the last of Paul's writings that remains to us.

9

Timeline of Paul's Ministry

(All dates are approximate, based on F.F. Bruce, *Paul: Apostle of the Heart Set Free*, page 475.)

Public ministry of Jesus	28-30 AD
Conversion of Paul (Acts 9:1-19)	33
Paul visits Jerusalem to see Peter (Galatians 1:18)	35
Paul in Cilicia and Syria (Galatians 1:21, Acts 9:30)	35-46
Paul visits Jerusalem to clarify the mission to the Gentiles (Galatians 2:1-10)	46
Paul and Barnabas in Cyprus and Galatia (Acts 13-14)	47-48
Letter to the Galatians	48?
Council of Jerusalem (Acts 15)	49
Paul and Silas travel from Antioch to Asia Minor, Macedonia, and Achaia (Acts 16-17)	49-50
Letters to the Thessalonians	50
Paul in Corinth (Acts 18:1-18)	50-52
Paul visits Jerusalem	52
Paul in Ephesus (Acts 19)	52-55
Letters to the Corinthians	55-56
Paul travels to Macedonia, Dalmatia, and Achaia (Acts 20)	55-57
Letter to the Romans	early 57
Paul to Jerusalem (Acts 21:1-23:22)	May 57
Paul imprisoned in Caesarea (Acts 23:23-26:32)	57-59
Paul sent to house arrest in Rome (Acts 27:1-28:31)	59-62
Letters to Philippians, Colossians, Ephesians, Philemon	60?-62
Letters to Timothy and Titus	?
Paul executed in Rome	65?

Saul the Pharisee

Paul was born in the first decade AD in Tarsus, a small but prosperous city on the trade route from Syria to Asia Minor. Tarsus was known for its schools of philosophy and liberal arts, and some scholars believe Paul must have had some contact with these. Like most cities in the Empire, Tarsus probably contained synagogues of Greek-speaking Jews who were often as devout as their Hebrew-speaking brethren.[1]

However, in Philippians 3:5, Paul calls himself "a Hebrew of Hebrews," which probably means that his parents spoke Hebrew and raised him in a strict Jewish home, isolated as much as possible from the pagan city around them.[2] They named their boy "Saul" after Israel's first king, for the family belonged to King Saul's tribe of Benjamin (Philippians 3:5). They must have owned property and had some importance in the community, for Saul was born not only a citizen of Tarsus (Acts 21:39) but also a citizen of Rome (Acts 22:27-28).[3]

Saul was sent to study Jewish law in Jerusalem under the foremost rabbi of his day, the Pharisee Gamaliel (Acts 22:3, Galatians 1:14). The word *Pharisee* comes from a Hebrew word meaning "the separated ones," for the Pharisees felt God had set them apart to live by the Law of Moses. Some Pharisees held that a man was righteous if he had done more good than bad, but Saul evidently followed the stricter group that insisted that every least implication of the law must be kept.[4]

The Pharisees expected a *Messiah* (Hebrew for "Anointed One"; Greek: *Christ*), who would deliver them from foreign oppression and rule with justice. However, Jesus of Nazareth had scandalized many Pharisees by interpreting the Law differently and claiming a special relationship with God. Thus, when some Jews began to proclaim Jesus as Messiah and Lord (a term usually reserved for God), strict Pharisees opposed them furiously.

Saul helped to lead the fight against the proclaimers of Christ in Jerusalem (Acts 7:58-8:3, Galatians 1:13). When some were driven out, Saul obtained permission to pursue them to Damascus. But on the way there, Jesus confronted Saul in a blinding encounter (Acts 9:1-19), revealing to Saul that he was persecuting the very God he professed to worship. Saul's life now turned from Pharisaic observance of God's Law to a devoted obedience to Jesus Christ, the revealed Messiah. He joined the Jews who were urging other Jews to believe in Jesus, and shortly thereafter God called him to proclaim Jesus as Savior to Gentiles (non-Jews) also. Saul took the Greek name Paul when he turned to work among Gentiles.

Paul the missionary

Paul's conversion may have marked his first move outward from cloistered Judaism into pagan culture. He spent ten years in Cilicia and Syria (Galatians 1:21), probably preaching Jesus along with Greek-speaking Jewish Christians. Then Barnabas called Paul from Tarsus to Syrian Antioch, where by this time the church was more Gentile than Jewish.[5]

11

Eventually, the church in Antioch commissioned Paul and Barnabas to evangelize Cyprus and Galatia. The two men traveled from Syrian Antioch to Cyprus, Pisidian Antioch, Iconium, Lystra, Derbe, and then back to Syrian Antioch (Acts 13:1-14:28, 2 Timothy 3:11). In Lystra they were nearly murdered by a mob, but they made some converts, among whom were a Jewish woman named Lois, her daughter Eunice, and Eunice's son Timothy.

Timothy

Since children of Jewish mothers are reckoned as Jews, Timothy could have been a full Jew. No doubt his Gentile neighbors regarded him so, and his mother raised him to know the Jewish Scriptures (2 Timothy 3:15). But Timothy's father was a Greek, and because of him Timothy had never been circumcised (Acts 16:1-3). Thus, despite his mother's lineage and his training in the Scriptures, Timothy was a Gentile in the eyes of Jews. His may have been a hard childhood for a sensitive boy, excluded by Gentiles for his Jewishness and by Jews for his uncircumcision.

But when he, his mother, and his grandmother became Christians, Timothy suddenly belonged to a group of people who didn't care whether or not he was a Jew. He belonged to people who shared together their neighbors' rejection and their Lord's promises. Timothy apparently flourished in his new identity, so that even Christians in Iconium, eighteen miles away, "spoke well of him" (Acts 16:2). When Paul returned to the churches he had planted in Galatia two years later, he resolved to take this impressive young disciple with him.

Timothy commissioned

Paul had another young man with him named Titus, a full Greek. Paul had not even considered circumcising Titus, for he felt strongly that the Jewish ritual law was not binding upon Christians (Galatians 2:3-5). But because Timothy was neither Jew nor Gentile, Paul decided that Timothy would be a more effective evangelist as a full Jew (Acts 16:3). Since circumcision was neither good nor bad to Paul (1 Corinthians 7:17-20), he chose to do what seemed most expedient for the gospel (1 Corinthians 9:19-23) and circumcised Timothy.

Before Paul left Timothy's home town, he also had the local elders lay hands on the young man to set him apart for his new ministry (1 Timothy 4:14, 2 Timothy 1:6).

Travels

Timothy accompanied Paul through Asia to Macedonia and Achaia (Acts 16:6-19:21), surviving riots, prison, and a criminal trial. During six years of traveling, Timothy learned enough to be trusted with a delicate mission to

Corinth, where factions and immorality were splitting the church (1 Corinthians 4:17).

Paul rejoined Timothy in Macedonia and traveled to Jerusalem, where Paul was arrested. As a Roman citizen, he appealed for a trial before the emperor, probably hoping to have Christianity officially declared a legal religion.[6] At this point, Timothy ceases to appear in the book of Acts; he may have gone on to strengthen the churches Paul's group had founded. When Paul wrote 1 Timothy, the young man was in Ephesus (1 Timothy 1:3).

Final days

Paul was probably released from his first imprisonment in Rome in 62 AD but was rearrested sometime later, perhaps in 65. He wrote 2 Timothy during this second imprisonment. Formerly he had been treated as a political prisoner, but now he was treated as a criminal. This time he was not simply restricted to a private house but locked in a dungeon and chained to a wall or a soldier.

Emperor Nero had his reasons for this change. Back in 60-62 AD when Paul was in Rome the first time, the Empire had been running well and Nero had been popular, for he had been leaving affairs of government to some gifted advisors. But between 62 and 65 Nero had replaced his competent servants and had begun to plunder the Empire to pay for his pleasures. The provinces—especially Judah—were groaning under his taxes, the economy was slumping, and Nero was in trouble with the Roman Senate for his murdering, licentious lifestyle. When a fire broke out in Rome in 64, Nero was suspected of arson. He found a scapegoat in an unpopular religious sect; Christians in the city were rounded up and thrown to animals—officially to pay for setting the fire but really to satisfy Nero's blood lust. The Roman people soon grew disgusted at this persecution, but it was unsafe to be a Christian in Rome as long as Nero lived, for he continued to need scapegoats for his crimes.

Thus, when Paul was rearrested, he became another pawn in Nero's game to survive politically. Paul wrote 2 Timothy from his dungeon cell shortly before he was executed.[7]

1. A. T. Robertson, "Paul, the Apostle," *The International Standard Bible Encyclopaedia*, volume 4 (Grand Rapids, Michigan: William B. Eerdmans Publishing Company, 1956), page 2276.
2. F. F. Bruce, *Paul: Apostle of the Heart Set Free* (Grand Rapids, Michigan: William B. Eerdmans Publishing Company, 1977), pages 41-43.
3. Bruce, pages 32-40.
4. Bruce, pages 50-51.
5. Bruce, pages 127-133.
6. Bruce, pages 443-444.
7. Josephus, *Antiquities*, 20.8.2; Josephus, *Wars*, 2.7.8; S. Angus, "Nero," *The International Standard Bible Encyclopaedia*, volume 4, pages 2134-2138.

OVERVIEW

Second Timothy is at once two extraordinary things: it is the last preserved words of one of the Church's greatest men; and it is God's Word to us, revealing who He is, who we are in Him, and what He desires from us. For the moment, take it as a letter from a man to his trusted friend. Approach it as you would a letter to yourself, not stopping to wrestle with individual phrases, but looking for the overall message.

First impressions

1. Read 2 Timothy at one sitting. How would you describe the *mood* (tone, emotion) Paul conveys? In other words, what seem to be Paul's attitudes or feelings toward his subject matter and toward Timothy? (Is Paul formal, intimate, angry, joyful . . . ?) If you think his mood changes, note where and how it changes.

   _____

   _____

   _____

   _____

   _____

   _____

For Thought and Discussion: In this letter, is Paul primarily teaching doctrine, exhorting, rebuking . . . ?

For Thought and Discussion: What impresses you most about Paul as a person in this letter?

2. Repetition is a clue to the ideas that are most important in a book. What words and ideas are repeated in each of the following sets of verses?

1:3,4,5,6 _____

_____

1:8,12; 2:3,9; 3:11,12 _____

_____

1:8,12,16 _____

_____

1:11; 2:2; 3:10,16; 4:2 _____

_____

other _____

_____

_____

_____

Study Skill—Cross-references
Other passages of Scripture can often shed light on the passage you are studying. These other passages are called *cross-references*.

3. What background information do you learn from the following verses concerning . . .

Timothy (1:5, 3:15)? _____

_____

_____

_____

how Paul feels about Timothy (1:2-4, 4:21)?

_____

_____

_____

Paul's circumstances (1:8,12,15-18; 4:6-18)?

_____

_____

_____

_____

Paul's feelings about Timothy, as shown in an earlier letter to a church (Philippians 2:19-22)?

_____

_____

_____

_____

Broad outline

If your impression of 2 Timothy is vague after one reading, a broad outline can help sharpen it.

Study Skill—Different Versions
The more times you read a book of the Bible, the better your understanding of it will be. Reading a different translation can help you notice new things and can make a confusing passage clearer.

---

4. Reread 2 Timothy, preferably in a different version. This time, think of a short phrase or sentence that can serve as a title for each paragraph. It may help you to include key words from the paragraph. Write your title below.

   (There is no one right answer; the first title is given as an example. Your Bible's paragraph divisions may differ, so feel free to alter those given here.)

1:1-2 _Apostle to Son_____

1:3-18 _____

_____

2:1-13 _____

_____

2:14-26 _____

_____

3:1-9 _____

_____

3:10-17 _____

_____

4:1-8 _____

_____

4:9-18 _____

_____

4:19-22 _____

_____

Theme/purpose

People usually write letters in response to a particular situation in their own or their readers' lives. They normally have reasons for choosing the topics they cover in their letters. Although it is often not possible to reconstruct the exact circumstances that prompted a letter, any insight in this area will help us to understand the writer's message.

Our own purpose for studying the letter will often differ from its original purpose, but how we understand and apply a writer's words should be influenced by how he and the Holy Spirit meant them to be understood and applied in the first century.

5. From your first readings of 2 Timothy, what seem to be Paul's chief aims in writing this letter?

_____

_____

_____

_____

_____

_____

6. If you have not already done so, read the historical background on pages 9-13. If you feel that
   additional background information would help
   you to better interpret Paul's letter, you might
   write down your questions here. Some of your
   questions may be answered later in this study
   guide. The sources on pages 81-85 may help
   you answer others.

   _____

   _____

   _____

   _____

7. Your overview of 2 Timothy may have suggested
   questions you'd like answered as you go deeper
   into the book. If so, jot them down now while
   your thoughts are still fresh. Your questions can
   serve as personal objectives for your further
   investigation of the letter.

   _____

   _____

   _____

   _____

Study Skill—Application
The last step of Bible study is asking yourself,
"What difference should this passage make
in my life? How should it make me want to
think or act?" Application will require time,

(continued on page 20)

(continued from page 19)

Optional Application: Choose one of the exhortations Paul gives to Timothy in this letter. Meditate on it during the coming week, and explore how you might apply it to yourself. (Read about meditating on page 7.)

Optional Application: a. How are you like and unlike Paul in this letter? How would you like to be more like him?

b. For the next week, ask God daily to make you more like Paul in this way. How would having this quality affect your actions?

thought, prayer, and perhaps even discussion with another person.

At times, you may find it most productive to concentrate on one specific application, giving it careful thought and prayer. At other times you may want to list many implications a passage of Scripture has for your life, and then choose one to concentrate on for prayer and action. Use whatever method helps you to remember application when you finish your study time.

8. From what you have read so far, do Paul's words seem to apply to any areas of your life? If so, what are some of those areas?

_____

_____

_____

_____

_____

For the group

This "For the group" section and the ones in later lessons are intended to suggest ways of structuring your discussions. Feel free to select what suits your group. The main goals of this lesson are to get to know 2 Timothy as a whole and to get to know the people with whom you are going to study it.

Worship. Some groups like to begin with prayer and/or singing. Some share requests for prayer at the beginning but leave the actual prayer until after the study. Others prefer just to chat and have refreshments for a while and then move to the study, leaving worship until the end.

Warm-up. The beginning of a new study is a good time to lay a foundation for honest sharing of ideas, to get comfortable with each other, and to encourage a sense of common purpose. One way to establish common ground is to talk about what each group member hopes to get out of your group—out of your study of 2 Timothy, and out of any prayer, singing, sharing, outreach, or anything else you might do together. If you have someone write down each member's hopes and expectations, then you can look back at these goals later to see if they are being met. Allow about fifteen to thirty minutes for this discussion.

Reading. It is often helpful to refresh everyone's memory by reading the book aloud before discussing your overview. Second Timothy should take about fifteen minutes to read. Have a different person read each chapter, asking those people to read with the tone or mood they think Paul was trying to convey, so that the letter sounds like the work of a living person.

First impressions. Ask the group to share first impressions of 2 Timothy—its style, mood, content, and so on. If members don't understand the question, you might ask them how Paul's letter is like and unlike letters they write, or like and unlike a sermon, a graduation speech, or advice from a father. The point of question 1 is to help the group see 2 Timothy as a real letter from one person to another person for a specific occasion. However, don't belabor this question, especially if it doesn't help your group.

The setting of a letter is an important part of the context of what it says, so question 3 helps you look for clues to the setting. The background on pages 9-13 may also help. See how much you can piece together from clues in the letter, without wild speculation, about why Paul wrote to Timothy and what was going on in their lives at the time.

Looking for repeated words and ideas (question 2) should help the group see themes and main ideas in Paul's letter. You might ask members to name as many repeated phrases and ideas as they can, and then move to the letter's themes (question 5). Then share your outlines (question 4). Remember that there is no one right way to outline 2 Timothy; a glance at a few commentaries or study Bibles will show you how widely the outlines of scholars differ.

Questions. Give everyone a chance to share questions about the letter or the way you are studying it. It is good to clear up confusion about the book, the group, or the study guide as early as possible. You may want to leave some questions about the book until later in your study; they may answer themselves as you go deeper if you are looking for the answers. You could point out the list of references on pages 81-85 or encourage members to seek answers from their pastors or other Christians they respect.

Application. Question 8 ties in with the expectations and objectives you discussed at the beginning of your meeting, but you may want to address it briefly now, after you have looked the letter over together. If some group members are unfamiliar with how to apply God's Word to their lives in specific ways, this might be a chance to think of some sample applications together. You could do this next week if you are running out of time.

Wrap-up. The group leader should have read through lesson two and its "For the group" section. At this point, he or she might give a short summary of what members can expect in that lesson and in the coming meeting. This is a chance to whet everyone's appetite, assign any optional questions, omit any numbered questions, or forewarn members of any possible difficulties.

You might also encourage any members who found the overview especially hard. Some people are better at seeing the big picture or the whole of a book than others. Some are best at analyzing a particular verse or paragraph, while others are strongest at seeing how a passage applies to our lives. Urge members to give thanks for their own and others' strengths, and to give and request help when needed. The group is a place to learn from each other. Later lessons will draw on the gifts of close analyzers as well as overviewers and appliers, theoretical as well as practical thinkers.

Worship. Many groups like to end with singing and/or prayer. This can include songs and prayers that respond to what you've learned in 2 Timothy, or prayers for specific needs of group members. Many people are shy about sharing personal needs or praying aloud in groups, especially before they know the other people well. If this is true of your group, then a song and/or some silent prayer and a short closing prayer spoken by the leader might be an appropriate ending.

2 TIMOTHY 1:1-14

Unashamed

Ever since he became a Christian, Timothy has been devoted to his mentor Paul. Now the mentor is chained in prison, and the young man faces a flock of immature Christians and a barrage of opposition on his own. On his own? Paul couldn't be with Timothy, but he knew what a fearful leader needed to hear.

Read 1:1-14 carefully, alert to the emotions Paul conveys. Look for the overall theme or message of the passage.

Study Skill—Connecting Words

Connecting words are clues to the logic in a passage. Connectives may show . . .

Time: *after, as, before, then, until, when, while;*

Place: *where;*

Reason: *because, for, since;*

Result: *so, then, therefore, thus;*

Purpose: *in order that, so that;*

Contrast: *although, but, much more, nevertheless, otherwise, yet;*

Comparison: *also, as, as . . . so, just as . . . so, likewise, so also;*

Source: *by means of, from, through.*

---

1. In the left column on the next page, list each instruction Paul gives Timothy in 1:1-14. Then, in the right column, summarize each resource or reason he gives for obeying the instruction.

23

instruction	resource/reason
1:6	. . . For this reason . . . (1:5-6)
	through . . . (1:6)
	for . . . (1:7)
1:8	by . . . (1:8; RSV in)
1:8	who . . . (1:9-10)
1:13	that . . . (1:14)
1:14	with . . . (1:14)

Apostle (1:1,11). Literally, "one who is sent"—a messenger, proxy, ambassador. In Jewish law, this was the *shaliach,* "a person acting with full authority for another" in a business or legal transaction.[1]

The early Church recognized certain men who had seen the risen Jesus as apostles—the leaders with highest authority regarding doctrine and policy. (See Acts 1:1-8, 6:1-6; Galatians 2:7-10.)

For Thought and Discussion: a. According to 1:1,11, what has God commissioned Paul to do?

b. How is this related to what God has commissioned Timothy to do (1:8, 2:2, 4:1-2)?

For Further Study: For more light on 1:6, 1 Timothy 4:14 applies specifically to Timothy; Ephesians 4:7-12 and Acts 6:1-6 apply more widely; 1 Corinthians 12:4-11 applies to Christians generally.

2. a. What is "the gift of God, which is in you" (1:6)? See 1:5,7.

_____

_____

_____

_____

b. What does it mean to fan this gift into flame (kindle it afresh; 1:6)? See 1:8.

_____

_____

_____

_____

_____

3. In 1:9-10, Paul outlines the gospel he has received from God and entrusted to Timothy. What key points does Paul mention? (Look for at least six.)

_____

_____

_____

_____

_____

25

For Thought and Discussion: How has Jesus "destroyed death" (1:10)? See Romans 3:23-25, 6:20-23; Hebrews 2:14-15.

_____

_____

_____

_____

_____

_____

_____

4. Why is it crucial that God "saved" and "called" us not because of anything we have done (1:9)? (*Optional:* See Ephesians 2:8-10, Titus 3:5.)

_____

_____

_____

_____

5. a. How does Paul explain "the promise of life" (1:1) in 1:10?

_____

_____

_____

b. This promise was important to Paul as he faced execution in Rome. Why is it important for you to focus on this promise?

_____

_____

_____

_____

26

Guard what I have entrusted to him (1:12). This phrase is more literally, "guard the deposit of me," and so it could mean either the deposit Paul has entrusted to God or the deposit God has entrusted to Paul.

If interpreted in the second way, the phrase means that God will guard the message He has given Paul, even if Paul falters or if the Church is persecuted. "Deposit" has this meaning—the gospel entrusted to Paul and Timothy—in 1 Timothy 6:20 and 2 Timothy 1:14.[2]

However, NIV and NASB think Paul would probably not have said "my deposit" in Greek if he had meant "the deposit given to me." Therefore, NIV and NASB interpret Paul to mean "the deposit of my soul (or salvation) that I have given to Him."

For Thought and Discussion: Think about the spirit we have been given (1:7). Why are power, love, and self-discipline all important for those who want to serve God?

For Thought and Discussion: Why does God guard the treasure in verse 12 and Timothy guard the one in verse 14?

For Further Study: Study Matthew 25:14-30 in connection with 2 Timothy 1:6,14.

6. a. In 1:12-14, Paul tells Timothy God's responsibility and man's. What deposit is God supposed to guard (1:12)?

_____

_____

_____

b. What good deposit (NASB: "treasure") is Timothy supposed to guard (1:14)?

_____

_____

_____

7. Paul tells Timothy to guard a treasure/deposit (1:14) and rekindle God's gift (1:6). Do you think you have been entrusted with any deposit? If so, what might it be?

_____

27

For Further Study:
Look up Ephesians
4:7 and Romans
12:4-6. What do
these scriptures teach
about the function of
each Christian in the
Church?

**Optional
Application:** What
are some implica-
tions of 1:7 for your
response to the chal-
lenge of testifying
and suffering? How
can you act on those
implications during
the next few weeks?

**For Thought and
Discussion:** If God
has called us to do
something, then what
can we assume
regarding the ability
and resources we
need to do it? (See
John 15:5; 2 Corin-
thians 3:4-6; Philip-
pians 2:12-13;
2 Timothy 1:6-8,14.)

_____
_____
_____
_____

8. a. Why might a modern Christian be tempted to
be timid toward testifying about Jesus?

_____
_____
_____
_____
_____

b. How might the gift named in 1:7 enable a
timid Christian to join in testifying and suffering (1:8)?

_____
_____
_____
_____

9. a. Of all that Paul says in 1:1-14, does anything
encourage you to dare to fan the flame of
your faith into greater exercise? If so, what
encourages you?

_____
_____
_____
_____
_____

28

b. Is there any way you might act on this insight during the coming week? Does this insight prompt you to talk to God about anything? Describe any prayer or action you might pursue.

_____

_____

_____

_____

_____

_____

Optional Application: Choose a verse or verses from 1:1-14 to meditate on during the coming week. For example, take five minutes each day to reflect on what 1:6-7, 1:9-10, or 1:13-14 implies for your life.

10. Reread 1:3-14. How would you summarize Paul's message in this passage?

_____

_____

_____

_____

_____

Study Skill—Outlining

One way to grasp the train of thought in a passage is to outline it. Your outline can be as brief or thorough as you find helpful. You might follow these steps to outline 2 Timothy 1:1-18:

1. Divide the passage into main sections, such as 1:1-2, 1:3-14, and 1:15-18. Try to see where Paul's train of thought shifts.

2. If necessary, divide the main sections into paragraphs. For instance, you might feel that 1:3-7, 1:8-12, and 1:13-14 are logical paragraphs. (Many Bibles suggest paragraphs for you.)

3. In a short phrase or sentence,

(continued on page 30)

For Further Study:
Try outlining 1:1-14.
You will get to 1:15-
18 in lesson two.

(continued from page 29)
summarize what Paul is saying in each paragraph. Try to follow his logic from paragraph
to paragraph.

4. Summarize each main section. A
summary of 1:3-14 should show the train of
thought through its three paragraphs.

11. If you have any questions about 1:1-14—about
what something means or how it applies to you,
for instance—write your questions here.

_____

_____

_____

_____

For the group

Worship

Warm-up. Instead of launching into the passage
immediately, you might begin with a question to
help members gather their thoughts. Some examples might be: "Has anyone ever been sent on a
mission? What happened?" Or, "Were you ever given
a message to relay? What happened? How did you
feel?"

Reading the passage. Have someone read 1:1-14
aloud before you begin discussing it. Even though
almost everyone has read the passage before, all will
probably benefit from a refresher.

Summary. It's often helpful to let several members
summarize the passage before you study it in detail.
You will probably come up with better summaries
after you have discussed the passage, but a quick
overview first will help you keep individual verses in
context.

Questions. Especially when the group has prepared
the study ahead of time, it often becomes dull to ask
repeatedly, "What did you get for number 1 . . . 2

. . . 3 . . . ?" Instead, you might reword or even reorder the questions.

To reword or reorder, you can use the observe-interpret-summarize-apply pattern. For instance, instead of saying, "What did you get for number 1?" you could ask, "What does Paul *say* in 1:6 that Timothy should do?" [Fan into flame the gift of God.] Then, "How would you *explain* this instruction *in your own words*?" Let several people respond to your interpretation question. Then have several people state and explain the reasons Paul gives for this instruction. Then, ask someone, "Jane, how would you *summarize* what we've said about fanning God's gift into flame?" Finally, ask, "Do these verses *apply* to us in any way? If so, how?" or "If not, why not?"

Sometimes a question in even the best study guide is unclear. When that happens, don't panic. Any question can usually be reduced to one of three questions: What can the passage tell us about who God/Jesus is? What can the passage tell us about who we are (as natural humans, as Christians)? And, what can the passage tell us about what God wants us to do, individually or together?

Don't oblige anyone to share personal applications, but encourage the group to do so. If members don't understand how to answer questions like question 9a-b of this lesson, you could brainstorm together some examples of how a person might answer those questions. Remember that the logic behind any application question is, "What does this passage tell us about who we are and what we should do this week?"

Question 5 on 1:10 may be difficult for some people. Have someone explain briefly how Jesus "destroyed death" by undergoing the death penalty for sin in our place and by rising sinless from the dead. It wasn't possible to include all possible cross-references for 1:10, but a commentary on 2 Timothy or Romans 3-6, or a Bible dictionary article on justification or atonement might help.

Second Timothy 1:12 is a problem because "guard the deposit of me" can be interpreted either as NIV or as RSV does. If you have group members who use RSV, question 6 may confuse them. Explain that question 6 follows the NIV interpretation, and discuss the implication of RSV's interpretation also.

Summary. Ask several people to summarize 1:1-14

again at the end of your discussion. These summaries may be much richer than those the group came up with at the beginning. You might also ask someone to summarize the key points of your discussion; the group's notetaker would be a logical person to ask.

Worship. Does God reveal anything about Himself in 1:1-14 for which you could praise Him, or anything He has done for which you could thank Him? Does the passage suggest anything you might ask Him to do, or to empower you to do? Is there anyone else—one of your leaders, for instance—for whom this passage moves you to pray?

1. Erich von Eicken and Helgo Lindner, "Apostle," *The New International Dictionary of New Testament Theology*, volume 1, edited by Colin Brown (Grand Rapids, Michigan: Zondervan Corporation, 1975), page 128.
2. Donald Guthrie, *The Pastoral Epistles* (Grand Rapids, Michigan: William B. Eerdmans Publishing Company, 1957), page 132; E. Edmond Hiebert, *Second Timothy* (Chicago: Moody Bible Institute, 1958), page 43.

2 TIMOTHY 1:15-2:13

Endurance

Paul gives Timothy no illusions that his Christian life should be easy or glamorous. Exhortations to "be strong" and "endure" punctuate 2:1-13, and the soldier, athlete, and farmer are suitable images of hard work. Still, Paul doesn't leave Timothy focusing on the work; the attitude, the purpose, and the future reward of devotion are as important as the work itself.

Study Skill—What's the Point?
In lesson two, you summarized 1:3-14 after studying it in detail. However, it can also help to look for a passage's main message before you study it in detail.

The key question here is, "What's the point?"[1] That is, 1) What is Paul talking about in this passage; and 2) Why is he saying it here (What does it have to do with what comes before and after)? In 2:1-13, for instance, Paul is not making random statements about Christ and Christianity. He has chosen what he says to make a point.

---

1. Read 2:1-13 several times. As you begin your study, what seems to be Paul's overall point in this passage?

   _____

   _____

For Thought and Discussion: a. What attitudes can keep a person from using the grace available to him (Galatians 5:4, Hebrews 4:16, 1 Peter 5:5)?

b. What attitudes toward one's work should result from working by God's grace?

2. In 1:15-18, Paul describes the actions of some Christians. Many have deserted him, but Onesiphorus has remained committed to Paul. Why do you think Paul inserted these comments and prayers between 1:1-14 and 2:1-13?

Grace (2:1). God's unmerited favor toward mankind, especially in 1) the gift of His Son to take away our sins and reconcile us to God (Romans 3:23-24, 5:1-21), and 2) the daily provision of the Holy Spirit's power for those who are united "in Christ Jesus" (Romans 8:1-17). This power enables us to remain in Christ, to do what He desires, and to become the people He desires.

3. Fulfilling the commission Paul describes in 2:2-13 takes supernatural strength—grace from God in Christ Jesus (2:1).

How does God's servant appropriate His grace?

34

For Thought and Discussion: What does 2:2 have to do with Paul's purpose in 2:1-13? With the letter's overall purpose?

4. God's grace makes possible the rest of what Paul urges in 2:1-13. Paraphrase the process he describes in 2:2.

_____

_____

_____

_____

_____

_____

5. a. How did Timothy learn to be a Christian leader?

   1:5, 3:14-15 _____

   _____

   _____

   1:2,13; 2:2; 3:10 _____

   _____

   _____

   b. In what ways does Timothy's training reflect the process in 2:2?

   _____

   _____

   _____

   _____

   _____

Endure hardship (2:3). RSV reads, "share in suffering," and NASB says, "suffer hardship." A related Greek verb (*sunkakopatheo*) is translated "suffer" in 1:8 and 2:9.

Endure (2:10,12). Unlike *sunkakopatheo*, this word *hypomeno* stresses the attitude of patient endurance rather than the suffering being endured.[2] Taken together, the two words express the treatment Christians should expect and the character with which they should respond.

6. How do Paul's exhortation to endure hardship and his three examples (2:3-7) relate to his instruction in 2:2?

_____

_____

_____

_____

_____

Study Skill—Similes and Metaphors
A *simile* is a figure of speech that uses "like" or "as" for comparison; "like a good soldier of Christ Jesus" is a simile. A *metaphor* sheds light on something by referring to it as something else—"All the world's a stage"—in order to imply a comparison between the two (usually dissimilar) things.
   Timothy is not a literal soldier or athlete, but the comparisons teach some key truths, if not taken too far. For instance, "a soldier of Christ Jesus" does not fight or kill unbelievers.

7. Paul urges Timothy to "endure hardship with us" (2:3), and then uses three similes to motivate his beloved son. What point is Paul making about Timothy's work with each of his three similes?
   To answer, first describe the characteristics

Paul says make a soldier, athlete, and farmer effective. Then explain how those characteristics apply to the Christian servant.

characteristic	application
soldier (2:4)	
athlete (2:5)	
farmer (2:6)	

For Thought and Discussion: a. What kinds of "civilian affairs" (2:4) can "entangle" (RSV) a Christian? How can we avoid such entanglement?

b. What "rules" might Paul have in mind in 2:5, and how do they apply to you personally?

8. Choose one of Paul's three similes in 2:4-6.
How does its lesson apply to you in your service
to God?

_____

_____

_____

_____

_____

9. a. Paul's own example should also motivate
Timothy. How would you describe Paul's attitude toward circumstances in 2:9-10?

_____

_____

_____

_____

_____

b. According to these verses, what convictions
enable and motivate Paul to have this
attitude?

_____

_____

_____

_____

_____

10. How should Christ's character, actions, and
promises encourage Timothy (2:8,11-13)?

_____

_____

_____

_____

_____

_____

_____

For Thought and Discussion: How does a person learn to teach and to train others to teach the gospel?

11. a. Where are you in the process Paul describes in 2:2? (For example, are you just learning to understand Paul's gospel? Are you ready to begin entrusting some of what you know to others? Could you train someone else to teach what you know?)

_____

_____

_____

_____

_____

b. What might be your next step toward becoming a well-grounded believer, qualified to proclaim the gospel and train others to do so?

_____

_____

_____

_____

_____

_____

12. In 2:1-13, what motivates you most to endure in serving Christ?

_____

_____

_____

_____

_____

_____

For Further Study:
Put together an out-
line of **2:1-13**, or
1:1-2:13, showing the
connections in Paul's
thought.

13. After studying the passage more closely, what
do you now think is Paul's overall message in
2:1-13? (Look at questions 1, 2, 4, and 6 on
pages 33-36, and consider how 2:1-13 relates to
1:1-18.)

_____

_____

_____

_____

_____

14. List any questions you have about anything in
2:1-13.

_____

_____

_____

_____

For the group

Warm-up. Try one of the following questions:
"Whom has God used to help you commit yourself
to Christ and mature in faith?" Or, "Have you ever
suffered ill-treatment for the sake of the gospel, or
do you know anyone who is suffering now?" (This
kind of testimony can be as encouraging to us as
Paul's was to Timothy.) Or, "In your experience,
what is the hardest part of living a Christian life?"

Read and summarize the passage.

Questions. It isn't clear what Paul means by "in the
presence of many witnesses" in 2:2. See some of the
commentaries on page 81 for more information. The
main issue in 2:2 (question 4) is the chain of
teachers entrusting "what you have heard from me"
(Paul's teaching, the gospel, "the deposit" of 1:14)
to the next generation.

Ask members to explain 2:1 (question 3) in
their own words. For instance, what does "the grace

that is in Christ Jesus" *mean*? How can we "be strong" in it?

Encourage everyone to make some application in question 8. You might need to help someone see that he or she already has a ministry to raise children, produce a worthwhile product, model Christian values to nonChristians, encourage other Christians in faith, or something else. Of course, don't force anyone to share his or her application with the group.

The convictions in question 9b are what Paul says is important to him, what he believes about God, what his goals are, and so on. All of these are in verses 9-10.

If question 11 seems difficult, you might first discuss how a person becomes a leader like Timothy. For example, he or she must first have a vital relationship with God. How does this happen? Then, he needs to know the facts of the gospel clearly enough to explain them to someone else. How could you help each other with this? Not every Christian is called to become a church leader, but everyone needs to be equipped for ministry (Matthew 28:18-20; Ephesians 4:7,11-12; 1 Corinthians 12:14-26; 2 Corinthians 5:16-20).

Question 12 should be a good relief from the challenge of question 11. Move to it as soon as you sense that people are finished with question 11.

The leader should never try to feed answers to the group; it is better to leave a question unanswered or to suggest where someone can go for an answer.

Summarize. This is a crucial part of your study. Help people see how 2:1-13 relates to 1:1-18, how 2:1-13 relates to Paul's overall message in 2 Timothy, and how 2:2 fits into the passage and the whole letter. Your group may be very inexperienced with seeing connections like these, but developing this skill should be one of your main objectives. Good Bible study is based on understanding the specific in light of the overall message.

It may also be helpful to have someone summarize how 2:1-13 applies to you. This may motivate group members actually to act on what they have learned.

Worship. Many commentators think 2:11-13 is part

41

of an early Christian hymn. You might choose songs and/or closing prayers with similar themes.

1. Gordon Fee and Douglas Stuart, *How to Read the Bible for All Its Worth* (Grand Rapids, Michigan: Zondervan Corporation, 1982), page 24.
2. Guthrie, pages 145-146.

2 TIMOTHY 2:14-26

A Workman Approved

So far, Paul has exhorted Timothy to guard the truth about Jesus that was entrusted to him (1:14), testify unashamedly to the truth about Jesus (1:8), entrust the truth to others who will pass it on (2:2), and endure suffering as he does all this (2:3). Paul has given reasons for perseverance in the face of fear and shame from hardship and rejection (1:5-2:13). The gift of God has been a theme (1:6-7, 2:1).

Now Paul turns to another problem Timothy must face—falsehood. As always, he focuses on the *character* of his dear son. As you read 2:14-26, consider how much of what Paul says is relevant to Christians who are not church leaders.

1. What seems to be Paul's overall point in 2:14-26?

   _____

   _____

   _____

   _____

   _____

2. Give one example of "quarreling about words" (2:14), "godless chatter" (2:16), or "ignorant speculations" (2:23 NASB) from your own experience.

   _____

For Thought and Discussion: a. Paul wants Timothy to remind the people he leads of "these things" (2:14). What are "these things"? (See 2:11-13.)

b. Why are these important for all Christians to remember?

For Thought and Discussion: Do you think 2:14,16,23 precludes debate or argument of every kind? If so, why? If not, what kinds of debate are acceptable for Christians?

For Thought and Discussion: Which of the actions you named in question 4 could someone who is not a pastor or elder practice?

Optional Application: How might the responses in question 4 have been applied to the experience you mentioned in question 2?

For Thought and Discussion: Think of someone you know who knows how to handle God's Word well. How did he or she become able to do that? (If you don't know, you might ask.)

3. According to 2:14,16,23, why should Christians avoid ignorant speculations and quarrels about words?

_____

_____

_____

_____

_____

4. How should a Christian respond to foolish arguments?

2:15 _____

_____

2:16,23 _____

_____

2:21-22 _____

_____

2:24-25 _____

_____

_____

5. a. What does it mean to "correctly handle the word of truth" (2:15)?

_____

_____

_____

_____

b. Name at least one step you could take to become better at handling the word of truth.

_____

_____

_____

6. What attitude does Paul want Timothy to have toward those who oppose him (2:24-26)?

_____

_____

_____

_____

_____

7. a. Why is it often hard to be kind, patient, unresentful, and gentle with quarrelsome people?

_____

_____

_____

_____

_____

b. How might you cultivate these attitudes toward others?

_____

_____

_____

_____

_____

Optional Application: How do you usually feel about and treat those who oppose you?

For Further Study: Look at Jesus' teaching and example regarding response to opponents. You could start with Luke 4:22-30; 5:21-26; 6:1-11,35-38; 7:36-50; 11:14-54; 15:1-7; 20:1-47.

For Thought and Discussion: What guidelines would you give a church for dealing with people in its midst who deny central Christian doctrines? Look for some guidelines in the New Testament.

For Thought and Discussion: Why is it wise to "flee" youthful lusts (2:22) but to "refuse" (NASB) foolish arguments (2:23)? What is the difference, if any?

That the resurrection has already taken place (2:18). Corinth also struggled with teachers who said that Christians experienced only a spiritual, not a physical, resurrection. Like Paul, they taught that a person died to sin, the old self, and the law, and was spiritually resurrected when he accepted Jesus as his Lord (Romans 6:2-11; 7:4,6). However, unlike Paul, they denied that a person would be resurrected as a whole—body, soul, and spirit—when Christ returns to judge the world. Paul wrote 1 Corinthians 15 to refute this teaching. He insisted that the hope of bodily resurrection and eternal life is at the core of the Christian faith (1 Corinthians 15:19).

Sealed with this inscription (2:19). "Having this seal" in NASB. Paul may be alluding to "the ancient practice of engraving inscriptions on buildings to indicate their purpose."[1] Paul likes to portray the Church as a building (1 Corinthians 3:9-17, Ephesians 2:19-22). Or, he may be speaking of the seal on a document that indicates "ownership, security, and authenticity."[2]

8. Even though chatter leads to foolish teaching and immorality, what confidence can a Christian leader have (2:19)?

_____

_____

_____

_____

9. a. What is Paul's point in 2:20-22?

_____

_____

_____

_____

_____

46

b. What does this point have to do with 2:16-19 and 2:23-26?

_____

_____

_____

_____

_____

10. Paul speaks of fleeing evil desires (verse 22) in the context of avoiding arguments and being prepared to counter false teachers in a godly manner. Can you think of any evil desires that might interfere with a person's effort to act as in 2:24-26?

_____

_____

_____

_____

11. How would you summarize 2:14-26?

_____

_____

_____

_____

12. Is there any area of your life that you would like to concentrate on for growth in light of 2:14-26? You might review your answers to questions 5 and 7b, or choose some other insight that motivates you. What prayer or action are you motivated to pursue?

_____

_____

_____

For Further Study: Make two lists from 2:14-26, one that shows "Traps to Avoid" and another "Traits to Acquire."

For Further Study: Outline 2:1-26 or 2:14-26, showing Paul's train of thought.

Optional Application: Choose a verse from 2:14-26 for memorizing and meditating.

47

_____

_____

_____

13. List any questions you have about 2:14-26.

_____

_____

_____

_____

For the group

Warm-up. Help the group focus by asking a simple starting question such as, "What do you usually do when someone starts a potential argument about Christian belief, practice, or lifestyle? Give each person a chance to answer, but let anyone pass who wants to.

Read and summarize. Have someone read 2:14-26 aloud, and then have several people summarize the train of thought in the passage.

Questions. Don't get into a long discussion of experiences from question 2; it is meant simply to help individuals identify with what Paul is saying. If someone remembers an experience that is clearly still painful, you might make an appointment to discuss and pray about it later. Someone may need to forgive people in his or her past, or to feel forgiven for his or her part in a quarrel.

On the other hand, one of these experiences may offer an example of how the responses of question 4 can work in practice. If no one wants to describe a real experience of a speculative or useless argument, you might invent a "case study" and apply the responses of question 4 to it. Concrete examples often help people to grasp a teaching.

When Paul mentions "the evil desires of youth" in 2:22, many people think first of sex, alcohol, and fast cars. Question 10 urges you to consider the context of this warning. Try rephrasing question 10 if the group has trouble with it. For instance, "How are these youthful lusts connected to foolish debates and quarrels? What character traits make young men (and other people) prone to arguments?"

Wrap-up. This might be a good time to evaluate how your meetings are going if you haven't done so before. You could just ask members to state or write down what they liked best about this meeting and what they liked least. Do this evaluation after someone has summarized 2:14-26 again.

Some kinds of application lend themselves to immediate action or prayer to begin letting God work on a habit. It can be helpful to share with the group how a particular verse has affected you, or how a particular plan of action has affected some area of your life. Both successes and frustrations can teach the group, suggest matters for prayer, and uncover possible solutions. This kind of updating is not a chance to prove who has grown most in the least time, but rather a chance to humbly give and receive help in growing. Sharing the results of our hardest efforts can help us not to rely on our own strength. You could set aside part or all of the next meeting to let each person share one application he has tried to make in the last month and how it is going. Or, you could set aside time at the beginning of each meeting and let those who feel moved to share do so.

Worship. The inscriptions in verse 19 suggest some themes for songs that you might look for. If you have been guilty of quarreling or condemning people who want to quarrel or teach falsehood, confessing your attitudes to God before the group may help you truly turn from them. You might also pray for any quarrelsome people you know according to 2:25-26, along with any prayers for your own needs.

1. Guthrie, page 150.
2. Hiebert, page 71.

2 TIMOTHY 3:1-9

Rejecters of Truth

In chapter 3, Paul advises Timothy on how to act in the "last days" as though Timothy will see them: "Have nothing to do with" the depraved religionists who will be abroad in those days (verse 5). Indeed, the Roman Empire was as full of such people as our world is, for the last days began at Jesus' first coming and will culminate at His return. For nineteen hundred years the Church has found the urgency in Paul's words relevant to current events.

1. Read 3:1-9. What is Paul trying to impress upon Timothy in this passage?

   _____

   _____

   _____

   _____

2. What does this warning have to do with chapter 2? (You summarized 2:14-26 on page 47.)

   _____

   _____

   _____

   _____

   _____

For Further Study:
Using a topical Bible or just leafing through one of the Gospels, explore Jesus' teaching on one of the traits listed in 2 Timothy 3:2-4.

3. The first two vices of verse 2 and the last one of verse 4 all point to the deluders' chief error: wrong love that corrupts potentially good things.

a. What should they love (verse 4)?

_____

b. What do they love (verses 2,4)?

_____

_____

c. How do people commit this error today?

_____

_____

_____

_____

Study Skill—Lists of Words

It's easy to skim over lists of traits like 3:2-4, getting a general impression of wickedness. We may feel that Paul is describing an especially depraved person, that we already know what such a person is like, and that the description doesn't apply to us. However, we can learn a lot about what we ourselves are like and what God desires us to be if we take time to ponder what these vices really mean. We can look up each word in a dictionary or compare how different Bible versions translate each word, and then write down a definition for each word or write down a word that means the opposite. Then we can ask ourselves whether we ever display such traits.

What to do when we fell convicted of having one of these traits is a deep subject. Prayer and reliance on God's Spirit to transform us internally are our chief tasks (1 John 1:8-10, Ephesians 3:16-19). But we also have a daily struggle to choose to agree with the Spirit (Romans 8:5-8, Ephesians 4:22-24).

4. For each of those vices in 2 Timothy 3:2-4, write down a word or phrase that describes its opposite, the trait a Christian *should* have.

boastful (RSV: proud) _____

proud (RSV: arrogant) _____

abusive (NASB: revilers) _____

disobedient to parents _____

ungrateful _____

unholy _____

unloving (RSV: inhuman, without natural affection)

_____

unforgiving (RSV: implacable, NASB: irreconcilable)

_____

slanderous (NASB: malicious gossips)

_____

without self-control (RSV: profligate)

_____

brutal (RSV: fierce) _____

haters of good things and people

_____

treacherous _____

rash (RSV: reckless) _____

conceited _____

Optional Application: Choose one of the good traits you named in question 3a or 4, and plan to be consistent in prayer about it. Ask God to cultivate that trait in you, and to show you ways of practicing it.

Godliness (verse 5). ". . . a personal attitude toward God that results in actions that are pleasing to God." "Devotion in action."[1]

Optional Application: Do you cherish any of the false loves Paul names in 2 Timothy 3:2,4? If so, how might the power of godliness (3:5) enable you to grow less attached to what you love more than God?

For Further Study: Jesus comments on "the form of godliness" in Luke 11:37-54, 12:1-3, 20:45-47. John 15:1-17 may shed light on the power of godliness.

For Thought and Discussion: Do women like the ones in 3:6-7 live in your community? If so, what can the Church do to help them resist clever deluders?

5. What is the power of godliness (verse 5)?

_____

_____

_____

_____

_____

6. What does "having a form of godliness but denying its power" (verse 5) tell you about the kind of religion the depraved ones practice?

_____

_____

_____

_____

_____

7. These people make their livings by exploiting the weaknesses of a certain kind of woman. Verses 6-7 describe such a woman's character. How would you paraphrase that description?

weak-willed _____

_____

_____

loaded down with sins _____

_____

_____

_____

swayed by all kinds of evil desires _____

_____

_____

_____

54

always learning but never able to acknowledge the truth

_____

_____

_____

Loaded down with sins (verse 6). This may mean that the women are so "overwhelmed in their consciences" that they clutch at any solution a clever person promises. They desperately want to be rid of guilt.[2]

Jannes and Jambres (3:8). According to Jewish commentaries of Paul's day, Jannes and Jambres were two of Pharoah's magicians who opposed Moses (Exodus 7:11).[3]

---

8. In what sense do men like those described in 2 Timothy 2:16-18 and 3:1-9 "oppose the truth" (3:8)?

_____

_____

_____

_____

_____

9. a. Does 3:1-9 offer any warnings you think you should take to heart? If so, what are those warnings?

_____

_____

_____

_____

_____

_____

For Further Study:
a. What is a depraved mind (3:8)?

b. Compare Paul's description of depraved people in 2 Timothy 3:2-8 to another in Romans 1:28-32. How are they similar and different?

c. What kind of mind should a Christian have (Romans 12:2, Ephesians 4:22-24, Colossians 3:1-3)?

b. Is there anything you plan to do, or ask God to do, about the warnings you have named?

_____

_____

_____

_____

_____

_____

10. List any questions you have about 3:1-9.

_____

_____

_____

_____

For the group

Warm-up. The beginning of a meeting can be a good time to share briefly how your efforts to apply 2 Timothy have been going. For example, have you been able to put anything you have learned into practice? If so, what has happened? If not, is it because nothing in 2 Timothy has seemed relevant, or for some other reason? If you committed yourself to pray about something in 2 Timothy, have you been faithful in doing so? If not, what seems to get in the way? Have you any questions about application that the group could answer or pray about?

In a brief (maybe 10-minute) discussion of this topic, group members can help remove roadblocks from each other's progress toward living out 2 Timothy (see Hebrews 10:24-25). But take care not to encourage performance orientation—the belief that God measures our worth by the good things we accomplish. Faithfulness is the important thing; you may not see results from your prayers, meditations, or actions for a while.

Read and summarize the passage.

Questions. You may want to expand on question 3, asking, "So, what does it *mean* to love God rather than self or pleasure? How does loving God affect what a person does?"

Questions 3 through 6 and the Study Skill on page 52 offer a chance to discuss how a person acquires godly character traits. If you do decide to discuss this, you should come prepared with scriptural backing for your views. *The Pursuit of Holiness* and *The Practice of Godliness*, both by Jerry Bridges, address this topic.

A quick way to cover question 4 is to go around the room and let each person name an opposite virtue for one of the vices. Strive for illuminating words like *humble, modest, honest, satisfied with God's praise,* rather than just *unboastful.*

You may want to have someone read the cross-references in the "For Further Study" question on page 54 ahead of time, especially if questions 5 and 6 aren't obvious. Be sure you grasp what godliness is before you discuss what its "form" and "power" are. You might simply ask someone to explain godliness in his or her own words, paraphrasing the definition on page 53.

Application should normally take up half your discussion time. The "For Thought and Discussion" question on page 54 suggests one way to apply verses 6-7, but you might think of another that better suits your group.

If you do discuss the "For Thought and Discussion" on page 54, remind the group not to name women that they consider weak-willed, since naming names can easily become slander.

After giving everyone a chance to respond to question 9, have someone summarize 3:1-9 and the main points of your discussion.

Worship. This indictment of an ungodly society may move you to pray for your own society. Remembering that we all have some of the traits in 3:2-4 should help inspire compassion for the kinds of people Paul describes. You may also want to ask God to deliver you from the faults Paul names.

1. Jerry Bridges, *The Practice of Godliness* (Colorado Springs, Colorado: NavPress, 1983), page 18.
2. Guthrie, pages 158-159.
3. Guthrie, page 159; Hiebert, page 88.

2 TIMOTHY 3:10-17

Timothy's Guides

In the last days between Christ's first and second comings, depraved people are going to be busy. But Timothy and all Christians like him have every resource they need to stand for Christ against wickedness.

As you read 3:10-17, look for the guides God has given us so that we can serve Him in difficult times.

1. Paul makes a series of "but" and "however" statements in 3:9-15. For instance, wicked men will try to cause trouble (3:1-8) *but* God will frustrate their aims (3:9). In 3:10-15 he goes on to contrast Timothy with the wicked men. What does Paul say?

But you (verses 10-11) _____

_____

_____

But they (verse 13) _____

_____

_____

But you (verses 14-15) _____

_____

_____

2. What seems to be Paul's overall aim in 3:10-17?

_____

_____

_____

_____

What kinds of things happened to me in Antioch
. . . (verse 11). Paul refers to what he endured
in his early days as a missionary. Timothy probably met Paul when the apostle first arrived in
Lystra (Acts 14:8-23). Some Jews had already
run Paul and Barnabas out of Pisidian Antioch
and Iconium for preaching about Jesus (Acts
13:13-14:7), but Lystra warmly welcomed the
missionaries until Jews from Antioch and Iconium arrived. The Jews persuaded the Lystrians
to turn against Paul and Barnabas. Then the
crowd stoned the men and dragged Paul's body
outside the city, presuming he was dead. But
Paul survived, and after spending some time in
Derbe he returned to strengthen the disciples in
Lystra. "We must go through many hardships to
enter the kingdom of God," Paul reminded the
Lystrian believers (Acts 14:22). These memories
of when Timothy and Paul first met must have
been fond and vivid for both men.

3. In 3:10-17, Paul reminds Timothy of two sets of
memories from his youth that should sustain
him when wicked people plague his ministry.
What should Timothy remember?

verses 10-11 _____

_____

_____

verses 14-17 _____

_____

_____

4. a. Why should Paul's words, lifestyle, goals, character, and experiences strengthen Timothy (3:10-11)?

_____

_____

_____

_____

_____

  b. Has anyone served as this kind of example for you? If so, how has that person strengthened your service to God?

_____

_____

_____

_____

_____

  c. Are you, or could you, model the Christian life for anyone as Paul did for Timothy? If so, for whom and how?

_____

_____

_____

_____

_____

5. a. Second Timothy 3:12 says that a committed Christian can expect persecution. Why is this so? (See 2 Timothy 3:13, John 15:18-25. You might also see James 1:2-4, 1 Peter 1:6-7.)

_____

_____

_____

For Thought and Discussion: List several of your personal convictions. How have you become convinced of them?

b. Think about why Paul inserted 2 Timothy 3:12 into the middle of contrasting Timothy with the wicked men. What is the connection between these ideas?

_____

_____

_____

_____

_____

6. Paul also wants Timothy to draw strength from what he has "learned and . . . become convinced of" (3:14). What is the difference between what you have _learned_ and what you have _become convinced of?_

_____

_____

_____

_____

7. On what has Timothy based his personal convictions (3:15-17)?

_____

_____

_____

All Scripture (3:16). "Scripture" means God's revelation written down. In Paul's time, Christians unanimously agreed that the Old Testament was Scripture. In addition, collections of Jesus' acts and sayings were regarded as Scripture by various groups of Christians, and one or two of our current Gospels may have been composed. Also, Paul had written many letters recording the revelation he had received from God, and some people—possibly Paul himself—regarded his writings as Scripture (2 Peter 3:15-16).

Thus, the "sacred writings" that Timothy has known from his youth are the Old Testament, but the "Scripture" that is God-breathed includes both the Old and New Testaments.[1]

God-breathed (3:16). "Inspired by God" in NASB, RSV. The Greek word *theopneustos* is composed of *theo*, meaning "God," and *pneustos*, which refers to breathing, blowing, or sending forth one's spirit. In the Bible, the breath, wind, or Spirit of God is closely connected with His creative Word and inspired speaking (Genesis 1:2-3, 1 Kings 19:11-13, Acts 2:1-4). When God breathed His Spirit into men so that they might be His spokesmen (prophets, writers of Scripture), He did not take over their minds or wills, but somehow guided them to speak His truth as they gave Him their attention.[2]

For Thought and Discussion: From 2 Timothy, would you say that Paul put his own teaching on a level with Old Testament Scripture? Why or why not (1:11, 13-14; 2:2; 3:10,14,16)?

8. a. What does Paul mean by calling Scripture "God-breathed" (verse 16)?

_____

_____

_____

_____

b. What are some the the implications of this fact for us?

_____

_____

_____

_____

_____

For Thought and Discussion: a. How does Scripture help us toward being saved (verse 15)?

b. How does it train us in righteousness?

For Further Study: For more on Scripture's help, see 2 Peter 1:3-4.

Optional Application: Meditate daily for the next week on Paul's example (verses 10-11), the uses of Scripture (verses 15-17), or verse 12. Memorize your chosen verses. What implications do those verses have for your life?

9. a. Paul lists five ways in which "God-breathed" Scripture is useful to us (3:15-16). Explain each in your own words.

giving "wisdom that leads to salvation" (NASB)

_____

_____

_____

teaching _____

_____

_____

rebuking _____

_____

_____

correcting _____

_____

_____

training in righteousness _____

_____

_____

b. What is the ultimate goal of using Scripture for these purposes (3:17)?

_____

_____

_____

10. Does anything Paul says about himself or Scripture encourage you in your current situation? If so, what encourages you?

_____

_____

Optional Application: Take time to thank God for the example of leaders like Paul and for the Bible. Thank Him for all the ways they help us.

For Further Study: Add 3:10-17 to your outline.

11. What implications, if any, does 3:10-17 have for *your* teaching, way of life, purpose, faith, or character?

_____

_____

_____

_____

_____

12. Why does Paul stress the importance of Scripture in the context of warnings about misleading, immoral teachers?

_____

_____

_____

13. List any questions you have about 3:10-17.

_____

_____

_____

_____

For the group

Warm-up. To start the group thinking, ask, "When it's difficult to persevere in your service to God, what is the one remembrance that most encourages you to keep going?" Or, "What is for *you* the hardest thing you have to endure in your ministry?"

Summary. Have someone read 3:10-17 first. Then have someone else briefly summarize each paragraph in the passage.

Questions. The logic of this lesson is as follows:

Overall structure and point of 3:10-17
　(questions 1-2)
Timothy's two guides (question 3)
　Paul's example (question 4)
　[aside on persecution (question 5)]
　Scripture (questions 6-9)
Application (questions 10-11)
Placing 3:10-17 in context (question 12)

As usual, the lesson moves from overview to verse-by-verse study to overview in context. Try to pace and guide the discussion so that everyone sees how Paul has organized the passage.

The most sticky part of this passage is question 8 on "God-breathed." You might want to research the topic in one of the books in footnote number one below. You might also want to mention in your discussion that question 8 is not a personal opinion, "everyone-is-right" question. Paul clearly has a specific meaning in mind, although Christians have argued about what that meaning is. If your group disagrees over the plain meaning of "God-breathed," you could ask your pastor or use a theological dictionary.

Worship. Songs and prayers thanking God for His Word or looking to the future Judgment would be appropriate for this study.

1. On the phrase, "All Scripture is God-breathed," see Benjamin A. Warfield, "Inspiration," *The International Standard Bible Encyclopaedia,* volume 2, edited by James Orr (revised edition by Geoffrey Bromiley) (Grand Rapids, Michigan: William B. Eerdmans Publishing Company, 1956), pages 1473-1483; William Evans and Coder S. Maxwell, *Great Doctrines of the Bible* (Chicago: Moody Press, 1979); Stephen Neill, *Jesus Through Many Eyes: Introduction to the Theology of the New Testament* (Philadelphia: Fortress Press, 1976); or another book you prefer.
2. Eberhard Kamlah, James D. G. Dunn, and Colin Brown, "Spirit," *The New International Dictionary of New Testament Theology,* volume 3, pages 689-708.

2 TIMOTHY 4:1-8

Passing the Mantle

When he left the world, Elijah gave his mantle to Elisha to signify that the young man who had served him would now succeed him as Israel's chief prophet (2 Kings 2:7-15). When a tired runner finishes his lap in a relay race, he passes the baton to a fresh runner and then goes to rest. Paul was not passing his apostolic status to Timothy, but he was passing on his task of guarding and spreading God's truth. As you read 4:1-8, sense Paul's emotion in his final charge to Timothy.

1. How does 4:1-8 relate to what Paul has been saying in chapters 1-3?

   _____

   _____

   _____

   _____

2. What does Paul urge in 4:2,5? (List as many of his exhortations as you can.)

   _____

   _____

   _____

   _____

   _____

For Thought and
Discussion: Does
what Paul describes
in 4:3-4 happen
today? If so, can you
think of some
examples?

_____

_____

3. In 4:1, Paul gives an incentive for these exhortations. How is this verse an incentive?

_____

_____

_____

_____

_____

_____

Preach (4:2). Declare as an ambassador would—
sensitively, diplomatically, yet also firmly and
authoritatively.

Correct (4:2). This word has the sense of motivating
the listener to confession or conviction of sin.

Rebuke (4:2). A pronouncement of reproof or blame
that requires humility and forgiveness, not con-
demnation (Mark 10:13,48; Luke 17:3).

Encourage (4:2). "Exhort" in NASB, RSV, KJV. To
remind a person of previously taught knowledge
in order to influence him to act upon it. Encour-
agement/exhortation addresses the intellect,
will, and emotions. Its methods range from a
gentle "you can do it" to an urgent "get mov-
ing!" The Greek verb *parakaleo* is related to the
noun *parakletos*, the title given to the Holy
Spirit in John 14:16. *Parakaleo* is literally "to
be called alongside" to help someone.

4. Why must Timothy preach patiently and sometimes reprovingly (4:2-4)?

_____

_____

_____

_____

_____

_____

5. What strikes you as especially significant in Paul's instructions of 4:2-4?

_____

_____

_____

_____

_____

For Thought and Discussion: What would it take for you to be able to say at the end of your life, "I have fought the good fight, I have finished the race, I have kept the faith" (4:7)?

Poured out like a drink offering (4:6). Along with the burnt offering of animal and grain, wine was poured around the base of the altar (Numbers 15:1-12; 28:7,24).

6. Paul compares his Christian life to a fight and a race. What similarities do you see among these?

_____

_____

_____

_____

_____

7. In 4:8, Paul returns to the same hope that he mentioned in 4:1. How is Paul's attitude in 4:6-8 an encouragement for Timothy?

_____

_____

_____

_____

_____

_____

8. How would you summarize 4:1-8?

_____

_____

_____

_____

_____

9. Which reasons in 4:1-8 most motivate you to serve with joy and endurance?

_____

_____

_____

_____

_____

10. a. In 4:2,5 Paul exhorts Timothy in several areas. Is there one in which you would like to be more faithful?

_____

_____

_____

_____

_____

b. What steps might you take toward improving in this area?

_____

_____

_____

_____

_____

11. List any questions you have about 4:1-8.

_____

_____

_____

_____

For the group

Warm-up. Ask, "Have you ever received someone's last words?" or "If you were about to be executed for your beliefs, to whom would you send your last words, and what would they be?"

Read and Summarize.

Questions. You could set the tone of this passage by asking the group what emotions Paul shows in 4:1-8, how he shows them, and why he feels that way. For example, why does he feel so strongly about what Timothy will do when he, Paul, is dead? When you make applications to yourselves (questions 9-10), try to identify with Paul's strong feelings about his and Timothy's mission and destiny.

Worship. Thank God for the work of Paul, Timothy, and others who have fought the good fight. Spend some time meditating on and praising God for the certainties Paul mentions in 4:1,8. Ask God to make those certainties as real and motivating to you as they were to Paul.

2 TIMOTHY 4:9-22 AND REVIEW

Personal Needs

In Paul's final words we get an intimate glimpse of the man's character, needs, and humanity. A warmly personal letter closes in that spirit, full of references to real people Paul and Timothy knew.

1. a. What do you learn about Paul's needs from 1:16-18 and 4:9-13,16?

_____

_____

_____

_____

_____

b. Do you have similar needs? Does someone you know have these needs? If so, how might you help see that they are met?

_____

_____

_____

_____

_____

Optional Application: a. Onesiphorus had a special ministry in Paul's life (1:16-18). Do you think it was as important as Timothy's? Why or why not?

b. How might you honor or pray for those who serve you like this? Or, how might you fulfill this ministry for someone else?

Optional Application: In what ways can you acquire and demonstrate attitudes like those Paul shows in 4:16-18?

2. What attitudes toward people and circumstances does Paul show in 4:16-18?

_____

_____

_____

_____

_____

Review

3. Reread all of 2 Timothy. It should be familiar to you by now, so you should be able to read rapidly, looking for threads that tie the book together. Pray for a fresh perspective on what God is saying.

   Also, review lesson one of this study, any outlines you made of 2 Timothy, and the summaries you made for each passage. This may sound like a lot of work, but it will help you remember what you've learned. Don't get bogged down; do what you can with the time and skills God has given you.

Study Skill—Returning to the Purpose
Many teachers of Bible study stress the importance of returning to the author's purpose after studying a book. J.I. Packer calls this the "spiral" approach to Bible study. Our view of the purpose often changes after a closer look. Even if our purpose for studying 2 Timothy is not the same as Paul's intent, his intent should affect how we interpret and apply what he says.

---

4. In lesson one, question 5, you said tentatively what you thought Paul's aims for this letter were. After closer study, how would you now summarize his main aims?

_____

_____

74

_____

_____

_____

_____

5. With this purpose in mind, make up a brief outline of 2 Timothy. (Your summaries of the passages on pages 29, 40, 47, 51, 60, and 70 may
   help you.)

6. What are the most important lessons you learned from 2 Timothy about . . .

God's character _____

_____

_____

_____

_____

_____

the Christian life _____

_____

_____

_____

_____

_____

the character of a Christian leader _____

_____

_____

_____

_____

_____

the responsibilities of a Christian leader _____

_____

_____

_____

_____

_____

_____

_____

_____

_____

obstacles to healthy church growth _____

_____

_____

_____

_____

_____

_____

reasons for godly leadership _____

_____

_____

_____

_____

other _____

_____

_____

_____

_____

_____

7. Review the questions you listed at the ends of lessons one through seven. Do any remain unanswered? If so, some of the sources on pages 81-85 may help. Or, you might study some particular passage with cross-references on your own.

8. Have you noticed any areas (thoughts, attitudes, opinions, behavior) in which you have changed as a result of studying 2 Timothy? If so, how have you changed?

_____

_____

_____

_____

_____

_____

9. Look back over the entire study at questions in which you expressed a desire to make some specific application. Are you satisfied with your follow-through? Pray about any of those areas that you think you should continue to pursue specifically. (Now that you have completed this study, perhaps something new has come to mind that you would like to concentrate on. If so, bring it before God in prayer as well.) Write any notes here.

_____

_____

_____

_____

_____

_____

_____

_____

_____

_____

_____

_____

For the group

Warm-up. To lead into question 1, try asking, "As you try to minister to other people, what is the biggest need you have that someone or some people might fulfill?"

Personal needs. Have someone read 1:16-18 and 4:9-22, and then give everyone a chance to respond to questions 1 and 2.

Review. It would probably help to refresh everyone's memory by rereading all of 2 Timothy together, either silently or aloud. You could allow five or ten minutes for everyone to skim the book.

Then, you might ask a few people to share their outlines of the book. They should tell what they think the purpose of book is, and how they see its major sections. Looking at several outlines at once, the group can discuss the merits of various views. Urge people to give their honest opinions with gentleness, and remind everyone that outlining and stating the book's purpose are probably the most difficult steps in Bible study. Commentators' outlines of 2 Timothy vary widely, since Paul probably did not construct his letter from an outline. Still, even a rough attempt to outline the book will help you understand and remember it.

If the group has trouble with question 6, you might point out some specific passages that teach on the various topics.

Give everyone a chance to raise unanswered questions, and take a few minutes to point the group toward answers. The leader should not answer the questions; rather, he or she should either let someone else answer them or suggest books or passages of Scripture that could answer them. It's a good rule never to do for the group what it can do for itself and grow by doing it.

Questions 8 and 9 allow you to evaluate your

growth as a result of studying and applying 2 Timothy. As was mentioned before, this is not a time to feel guilty or self-satisfied, but a time to be encouraged, remotivated, and enabled to keep going. If you don't see many results yet, do ask yourselves whether you should do or pray or think about anything differently, but don't assume that you should. You may just need to persevere in what you are doing and trust God for results.

Evaluation. You might take a few minutes or a whole meeting to evaluate how your group functioned during your study of 2 Timothy. Some questions you might ask are:

> What did you learn about small group study?
> How well did the study help you grasp
>   2 Timothy?
> What were the most important truths you dis-
>   covered together about the Lord?
> What did you like best about your meetings?
> What did you like least? What would you
>   change?
> How well did you meet the goals you set at
>   your first meeting?
> What are members' current needs? What will
>   you do next?

Worship. Thank God for specific things He has taught you and specific ways He has changed you through 2 Timothy. Thank Him also for the opportunity to study the Bible together. What songs seem appropriate to close a study of 2 Timothy?

STUDY AIDS

For further information on the material covered in this study, consider the following sources. If your local bookstore does not have them, ask the bookstore to order them from the publisher, or find them in a seminary library. Many university and public libraries will also carry these books.

Commentaries on Second Timothy

Fee, Gordon. *1 and 2 Timothy, Titus* (Harper Good News Commentary, Harper and Row, 1984).
    Brief, non-technical, verse-by-verse commentary for laymen. Mainly exegesis (explanation of the text), rather than exposition (preaching and application). Based on the Good News Bible, and grounded in sound scholarship to show the Greek behind the translation.

Guthrie, Donald. *The Pastoral Epistles* (Tyndale New Testament Commentary, Eerdmans, 1957).
    Like Fee's book, except that Guthrie's is based on the King James Version. Guthrie also did the excellent short article on 2 Timothy in the *New Bible Commentary: Revised* (Eerdmans, 1970).

Kelly, J. N. D. *A Commentary on the the Pastoral Epistles* (Baker, 1963).
    More thorough discussions than Fee or Guthrie. Very readable and not lengthy, although Kelly includes in parentheses the ancient sources for his explanations of the text and Paul's world.

Historical Sources

Bruce, F. F. *New Testament History* (Doubleday, 1979).
    A history of Herodian kings, Roman governors, philosophical

schools, Jewish sects, Jesus, the early Jerusalem church, Paul, and early gentile Christianity. Well documented with footnotes for the serious student, but the notes do not intrude.

Bruce, F. F. *Paul, Apostle of the Heart Set Free* (Eerdmans, 1977).
Possibly the best book around on the historical background and chronology of Paul's life. Bruce explains Paul's personality and thought from an evangelical perspective, although some readers will disagree with his interpretation at points.

Harrison, E. F. *Introduction to the New Testament* (Eerdmans, 1971).
History from Alexander the Great—who made Greek culture dominant in the biblical world—through philosophies, pagan and Jewish religion, Jesus' ministry and teaching (the weakest section), and the spread of Christianity. Very good maps and photographs of the land, art, and architecture of New Testament times.

Concordances, Dictionaries, and Handbooks

A *concordance* lists words of the Bible alphabetically along with each verse in which the word appears. It lets you do your own word studies. An *exhaustive concordance* lists every word used in a given translation, while an *abridged* or *complete* concordance omits either some words, some occurrences of the word, or both.

The two best exhaustive concordances are *Strong's Exhaustive Concordance* and *Young's Analytical Concordance to the Bible*. Both are available based on the King James Version of the Bible and the New American Standard Bible. *Strong's* has an index by which you can find out which Greek or Hebrew word is used in a given English verse. *Young's* breaks up each English word it translates. However, neither concordance requires knowledge of the original language.

Among other good, less expensive concordances, *Cruden's Complete Concordance* is keyed to the King James and Revised Versions, and *The NIV Complete Concordance* is keyed to the New International Version. These include all references to every word included, but they omit "minor" words. They also lack indexes to the original languages.

A **Bible dictionary** or **Bible encyclopedia** alphabetically lists articles about people, places, doctrines, important words, customs, and geography of the Bible.

The New Bible Dictionary, edited by J. D. Douglas, F. F. Bruce, J. I. Packer, N. Hillyer, D. Guthrie, A. R. Millard, and D. J. Wiseman (Tyndale, 1982) is more comprehensive than most dictionaries. Its 1300 pages include quantities of information along with excellent maps, charts, diagrams, and an index for cross-referencing.

Unger's Bible Dictionary by Merrill F. Unger (Moody, 1979) is equally good and is available in an inexpensive paperback edition.

The *Zondervan Pictorial Encyclopedia* edited by Merrill C. Tenney (Zondervan, 1975, 1976) is excellent and exhaustive, and is being revised and updated in the 1980's. However, its five 1000-page volumes are a financial investment, so all but very serious students may prefer to use it at a church, public, college, or seminary library.

Unlike a Bible dictionary in the above sense, *Vine's Expository Dictionary of New Testament Words* by W. E. Vine (various publishers) alphabetically lists major words used in the King James Version and defines each New Testament Greek word that KJV translates with that English word. Vine's lists verse references where that Greek word appears, so that you can do your own cross-references and word studies without knowing any Greek.

Vine's is a good basic book for beginners, but it is much less complete than other Greek helps for English speakers. More serious students might prefer *The New International Dictionary of New Testament Theology*, edited by Colin Brown (Zondervan) or *The Theological Dictionary of the New Testament* by Gerhard Kittel and Gerhard Friedrich, abridged in one volume by Geoffrey W. Bromiley (Eerdmans).

A *Bible atlas* can be a great aid to understanding what is going on in a book of the Bible and how geography affected events. Here are a few good choices:

The MacMillan Atlas by Yohanan Aharoni and Michael Avi-Yonah (MacMillan, 1968, 1977) contains 264 maps, 89 photos, and 12 graphics. The many maps of individual events portray battles, movements of people, and changing boundaries in detail.

The New Bible Atlas by J. J. Bimson and J. P. Kane (Tyndale, 1985) has 73 maps, 34 photos, and 34 graphics. Its evangelical perspective, concise and helpful text, and excellent research make it a very good choice, but its greatest strength is its outstanding graphics, such as cross-sections of the Dead Sea.

The Bible Mapbook by Simon Jenkins (Lion, 1984) is much shorter and less expensive than most other atlases, so it offers a good first taste of the usefulness of maps. It contains 91 simple maps, very little text, and 20 graphics. Some of the graphics are computer-generated and intriguing.

The Moody Atlas of Bible Lands by Barry J. Beitzel (Moody, 1984) is scholarly, very evangelical, and full of theological text, indexes, and references. This admirable reference work will be too deep and costly for some, but Beitzel shows vividly how God prepared the land of Israel perfectly for the acts of salvation He was going to accomplish in it.

A *handbook* of bible customs can also be useful. Some good ones are *Today's Handbook of Bible Times and Customs* by William L. Coleman (Bethany, 1984) and the less detailed *Daily Life in Bible Times* (Nelson, 1982).

For Small Group Leaders

How to Lead Small Group Bible Studies (NavPress, 1982).
    Just 71 pages. It hits the highlights of how to get members

acquainted, ask questions, plan lessons, deal with interpersonal relations, and handle prayer.

The Small Group Leader's Handbook by Steve Barker et al. (InterVarsity, 1982).

Written by an InterVarsity small group with college students primarily in mind. It includes more than the above book on small group dynamics and how to lead in light of them, and many ideas for worship, building community, and outreach. It has a good chapter on doing inductive Bible study.

Getting Together: A Guide for Good Groups by Em Griffin (InterVarsity, 1982).

Applies to all kinds of groups, not just Bible studies. From his own experience, Griffin draws deep insights into why people join groups; how people relate to each other; and principles of leadership, decision-making, and discussions. It is fun to read, but its 229 pages will take more time than the above books.

You Can Start a Bible Study Group by Gladys Hunt (Harold Shaw, 1984).

Builds on Hunt's thirty years of experience leading groups. This book is wonderfully focused on God's enabling. It is both clear and applicable for Bible study groups of all kinds.

The Small Group Letter (NavPress).

Unique. Its six pages per issue, ten issues per year are packed with practical ideas for asking questions, planning Bible studies, leading discussions, dealing with group dynamics, encouraging spiritual growth, doing outreach, and so on. It stays up to date because writers always discuss what they are currently doing as small group members and leaders. To subscribe, write to *The Small Group Letter*, Subscription Services, Post Office Box 54470, Boulder, Colorado 80323-4470.

Bible Study Methods

Braga, James. *How to Study the Bible* (Multnomah, 1982).

Clear chapters on a variety of approaches to Bible study: synthetic, geographical, cultural, historical, doctrinal, practical, and so on. Designed to help the ordinary person without seminary training to use these approaches.

Fee, Gordon, and Douglas Stuart. *How to Read the Bible For All Its Worth* (Zondervan, 1982).

After explaining in general what interpretation (exegesis) and application (hermeneutics) are, Fee and Stuart offer chapters on interpreting and applying the different kinds of writing in the Bible: Epistles, Gospels, Old Testament Law, Old Testament narrative, the Prophets, Psalms, Wisdom, and Revelation. Fee and Stuart also suggest good commentaries on each biblical book. They write as evangelical scholars who personally recognize Scripture as God's Word for their daily lives.

Jensen, Irving L. *Independent Bible Study* (Moody, 1963), and *Enjoy Your Bible* (Moody, 1962).

The former is a comprehensive introduction to the inductive Bible study method, expecially the use of synthetic charts. The latter is a simpler introduction to the subject.

Wald, Oletta. *The Joy of Discovery in Bible Study* (Augsburg, 1975).

Wald focuses on issues such as how to observe all that is in a text, how to ask questions of a text, how to use grammar and passage structure to see the writer's point, and so on. Very helpful on these subjects.